HANG-GLIDING & PARAGLIDING

by Noel Whittall

ticktock

The author

Noel Whittall started flying in 1973 with a home-built hang-glider. He went on to become Chairman of the British Hang-gliding Association.

Noel has written several books about the different aspects of hang-gliding. He is based in the north of England but travels extensively in Europe, flying for his own pleasure or judging at international competitions.

With thanks to: David Wootton, Diana LeCore and Anna Brett

Thank you to Lorraine Petersen and the members of nasen

ISBN-13: 978 1 84898 138 6 pbk
This revised edition published in 2010 by *ticktock* Media Ltd

Printed in China
9 8 7 6 5 4 3 2 1

Copyright © *ticktock* Entertainment Ltd 2008, 2010
First published in Great Britain as part of the series *Xtreme Sports* in 2008 by *ticktock* Media Ltd,
103 Goods Station Road, Tunbridge Wells, Kent, TN1 2DP

Picture credits (t=top; b=bottom; c=centre; l=left; r=right; OFC=outside front cover):
Age Fotostock/Superstock: 56b. David Bagley/Alamy: 34/35. Denis Balibouse: 48/49t, 58. Denis Balibouse/Red Bull Photofiles: 24/25, 44/45, 48b. Bettmann/Corbis: 10/11t. Elizabeth Czitronyi/Alamy: 57t. Steve Elkins: 19b. Flybubble Paragliding School, www.flybubble.co.uk: 29t. Getty Images: 9t, 9b. Ulrich Grill/Red Bull Photofiles: 31tr. John Heiney: 59b. INSADCO Photography/Alamy: 42t. Vitek Ludvik/Red Bull Photofiles: 28. Alfredo Martinez/Red Bull Photofiles: 20/21. Mary Evans Picture Library: 7c. Ian Mills, 10fifty.com: 15tr. Paraglidingshop.co.uk: 33t. Christian Pondella/Red Bull Photofiles: 49b. Francois Portmann/Red Bull Photofiles: 51c. The Print Collector/Alamy: 8. Bill Ross/Corbis: 29b. Pasi Salminen/Red Bull Photofiles: 51tr. Shutterstock: OFC, 1, 3, 4/5, 12/13, 14t, 15cl, 16, 17t, 17b, 20b, 22, 23bl x 3, 27 all, 32, 43tr. Bernhard Spöttel/Red Bull Photofiles: 46. Square1.com: 33br. Noel Whittall: 2, 10b, 11b, 18/19, 26, 37b, 38, 39t, 39b, 40/41t, 40b, 41b, 43bl, 47t, 47b, 50t, 53br, 57c, 59t, 60. Wikipedia: 36/37t. Wingsofrogallo.org: 23tr. David Wootton: 6/7t, 17c, 30t, 33c, 52cr, 52/53t, 54/55. Tim Wright/Corbis: 36b.

CONTENTS

CHAPTER 1: FIRST FLIGHTS

Gliding is one of the most extreme sports out there.

OVERVIEW

Nearly 1,500 years ago in China, people first tried flying. Many people were hurt or killed trying to fly.

Then in the 1900s, people who wanted to fly began studying birds. They realized that gliding birds do not need to flap their wings to fly.

HANG-GLIDING & PARAGLIDING

People began hang-gliding in the 1960s. Paragliders followed in the 1980s.

Hang-gliders have stiff wings. Paragliders are soft, like parachutes.

An early attempt at flying

EARLY HISTORY

Otto Lilienthal in a test flight

HANG-GLIDING & PARAGLIDING

Otto Lilienthal, Germany

The first great hang-glider was Otto Lilienthal.

He made wings out of wood and canvas in the 1880s. He hung from his glider by his armpits.

Chanute's assistant, Augustus Moore Herring, flying the biplane glider

Octave Chanute, USA

In 1896 Octave Chanute built a biplane glider. His assistant tested the glider on sand dunes by Lake Michigan, USA. A biplane has two wings.

THE FIRST GLIDERS

The Wright brothers built and flew the first aircraft in 1903. This flight took place in Kitty Hawk, North Carolina, USA.

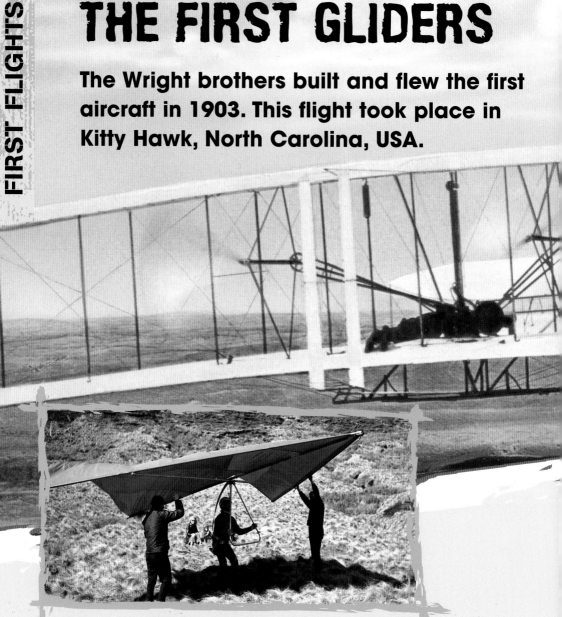

An early Rogallo glider

In the 1950s, American Dr Francis Rogallo invented parachutes for spacecraft. His ideas were used to create hang-gliders. These were called 'Rogallos'.

The modern hang-glider was invented in 1963 by Australian John Dickenson.

HANG-GLIDING & PARAGLIDING

Wilbur Wright watches Orville Wright

An early ram-air parachute

The paraglider

In 1978 a group of Frenchmen began jumping off mountains in a new type of parachute. They called it the ram-air parachute.

Companies began making these parachutes and named them paragliders.

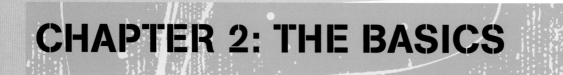

CHAPTER 2: THE BASICS

Hang-gliders are usually launched by running off a hill or mountain. They can also be towed into the air by an aircraft.

leading
edge

HOW GLIDERS FLY

Gliders do not need a motor. They use the rising air to fly. Rising air is called lift.

The large wing of a glider keeps its front (leading) edge tilted up higher than its back (trailing) edge as it flies. This means air is pushed downwards. The wing reacts to this by trying to rise.

**trailing
edge**

There are three types of natural lift.

Ridge lift: When wind meets a hill, it is forced upwards. This ridge lift helps pilots to climb higher.

Thermal lift: Thermals are patches of air that have been made extra warm by the sun. Thermals can take gliders up very high.

Wave lift: This happens when wind flows down the back of one hill and is 'bounced' up when it meets the front of the next hill. Wave lift is smooth and powerful.

Staying up

A glider needs to push downhill all the time to stay up. This is like riding a bike without pedals!

CONTROLLING A GLIDER

All aircraft use three types of movement: roll, pitch and yaw. Hang-glider pilots swing their bodies to keep control.

HANG-GLIDING & PARAGLIDING

Roll

Roll means tilting one wing lower than the other. The pilot tilts the wing by shifting their body sideways. This causes the glider to turn.

Pitch

Pitch means tilting the front of the glider up or down. This controls the speed. Pulling forwards speeds the glider up. Pushing back slows it down.

Yaw

Yaw is when one side of the glider is moved forwards, causing the glider to turn. When the right-hand side of the glider is moved forwards, the glider moves to the left.

THE HANG-GLIDER

Batten

Wing

Control frame

Bar

This is the basic set-up of a hang-glider.

The **wing** material fits over the main frame. It is called the sail. Several ribs, called **battens**, are sewn into each side.

The **hang point** is a strong loop on the **keel** at the centre of the **control frame**.

HANG-GLIDING & PARAGLIDING

Hang point

Carabiner

Keel

Harness

Quick-release catches make the glider easy to put together for flight

The **harness** joins to the hang point with a **carabiner**. The carabiner carries the pilot's weight.

Canopy

THE PARAGLIDER

Paraglider wings are inflated with air. This is called the ram-air effect. The wings are called canopies.

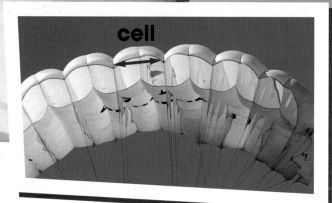

cell

The **canopy** is built from many cells that are sewn together side by side.

Each cell is open at the front and closed at the back.

The pilot sits in a **harness** that is attached to the canopy by many lines.

HANG-GLIDING & PARAGLIDING

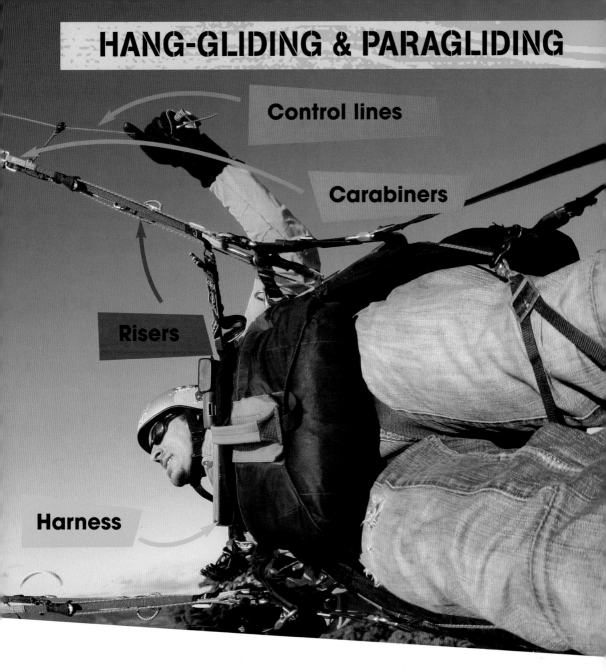

Control lines

Carabiners

Risers

Harness

The lines come together close to the pilot and are joined to short strips of webbing called **risers**.

The risers are attached to the harness with small **carabiners**.

The **control lines** are usually called brakes. The brakes help the pilot to yaw the canopy.

21

LAUNCHING AND LANDING

Both types of glider are challenging to handle. Launching and landing can be especially difficult.

Some display pilots use flares to mark their movements in the sky

Landing

To land a hang-glider, the pilot first slows the wing. Next they hold the sides of the control frame to slow it down.

Launching

The trickiest part of paragliding is launching.

First the wing is laid out on the ground. Then the lines are pulled to let in air. Finally, the risers are pulled to make the wing rise.

23

Gliding sports are dangerous. Pilots must have the correct equipment to help them to cope with the the changing conditions in the sky.

CLOTHING

Hang-gliding pilots need to dress for cold conditions, even though it may be warm on the ground.

High climbers

The higher gliders go, the colder the air becomes. Gliders can reach 4,500 metres. At this height, the average temperature is –17 degrees Celsius.

HANG-GLIDING & PARAGLIDING

Helmet

A helmet is a must. Head injuries can be very serious. For high flights, a warm hat is worn under the helmet.

Goggles

Sunglasses or goggles are essential. Eye-damaging UV rays in sunlight are much stronger very high up.

Flying suit

A one-piece flying suit is worn for paragliding.

Hang-glider pilots fly in warm harnesses, so they usually just wear windproof jackets.

EXTRA PROTECTION

Pilots also need the following equipment for protection.

Speedy arms

To make themselves go faster, pilots wear tight Lycra sleeves over their flying clothes. This keeps down the drag from their bodies.

HANG-GLIDING & PARAGLIDING

Warm hands and feet

Gloves or mittens need
to be worn whatever the
weather. Without gloves,
it is easy to hurt your
hands on the control lines.

Good boots are needed
to protect the feet.

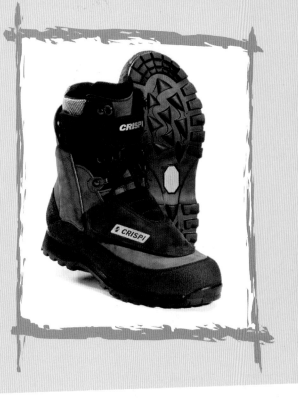

Sun protection

Always use strong sunscreen as the sun can
easily burn you.

Altimeter, variometer and GPS

EQUIPMENT

Pilots carry many instruments so they don't get lost.

A hang-glider pilot lies in the harness and has the instruments on the control frame.

Paragliders have the instruments in a waist pack that is clipped to the harness.

GPS

Combined vario/altimeter

Pilots carry a special map that shows airports and routes, called airways.

Here is a list of intruments:

Altimeter Shows the glider's height.

Variometer ('vario') Shows how fast the glider is climbing or sinking. It is dangerous to rise too fast or high.

GPS Shows the glider's route.

Two-way radio Sends out emergency signals.

It is important that glider pilots keep clear of airways that aeroplanes might be on.

SAFETY

Gliding accidents happen often. Most pilots carry a rescue parachute which is only used in a real emergency.

The rescue chute is joined to the glider by a strong line called a strop.

Landing protection

Landings can go wrong, so harnesses have built-in safety features. One safety feature is a thick layer of foam to protect the pilot's spine.

The spine protection is built in to the back.

Landings can cause serious injuries. When landing, pilots must keep their feet together and knees bent.

In wooded areas, pilots carry a long cord to help them climb down if they land in a tree!

A knife with a protected blade to cut away the parachute if needed

Today, there are gliders for beginners and professionals.

Students on their early flights are kept close to the ground by instructors using ropes

TYPES OF GLIDER

Competition and training gliders are flown in the same way. But competition gliders can go much faster.

In competitions, the aim is to fly a route across country as quickly as possible. Pilots have to find lots of areas of rising air (lift).

A competition glider being tow-launched by a microlight tug

The fast glide is good when flying from one area of lift to another.

A very stiff wing is faster but is difficult to turn. Pilots use a cord to help them to turn.

The stiffer the wing, the faster the glider

THE SWIFT

The Swift is a special type of hang-glider. It has extremely stiff wings and extra flaps on the wings to steer it like a plane.

Swift pilots sit in small cockpits with a door in the bottom. Swifts can be launched like other hang-gliders. Once they are off the ground, the pilots pull their legs up, close the door and control the Swift with a joystick.

Swifts are not easy to carry. The wings cannot be rolled up. It takes two people to launch a Swift.

Spoilers

RIGIDS

The rigid came along in the early 1990s.
It has a carbon-fibre frame. The rigid is
very light and strong, with a very stiff wing.

When the pilot swings sideways, he operates
flaps called spoilers on top of the wings. When
a spoiler lifts up, the glider turns to that side.

Spars

Ribs

A rigid is strong because of its long carbon-fibre spars and ribs.

TYPES OF PARAGLIDER

There are training paragliders and competition gliders. Training gliders are slow and stable. Competition gliders are fast, but hard to fly.

A training paraglider

A competition paraglider

Here are the main features of a competition glider:

- The canopy is wider and thinner.

- There are more cells in the canopy.

- The cells are smaller.

- The lines are much thinner. This helps with the wind.

- There is a foot-operated bar for more speed.

- The harness is slightly curved.

A wing tip collapsing

Competition gliders are flown only by experts at events like the World Championships.

CHAPTER 5: COMPETITION

The pilots in a cross-country paragliding competition have about an hour to find good lift and gain height. Then, the clock starts. Now the pilots have to race to the finishing line.

GLIDER CONTESTS

The starting age for hang-gliding and paragliding competitions is 16.

There are several types of contests for gliders: cross-country racing, landing accuracy, aerobatics, speed flying and record breaking.

Hang-gliders reach the inflatable finishing line after a speed race

HANG-GLIDING & PARAGLIDING

Cross-country racing

The competitors record their flights on their GPS instruments. Every competitor's flight is downloaded from their GPS to work out how well they've done.

Landing-accuracy competitions

For this competition, pilots have to make a stand-up landing on a target.

Hitting the spot is much harder than it looks, especially if the wind is strong.

AEROBATICS

Aerobatic (acro) flying on hang-gliders or paragliders is a very special skill.

Acro competitions usually take place over a lake.

Pilots are scored for the difficulty of the things they do and on how good they look in the air.

An acro pilot landing on a raft in a lake

*Othar Lawrence
performing
a wing-over*

Each trick has a special name. Some tricks involve loops and high-speed spirals.

The first Acro World Championships were near Montreux, Switzerland, in 2005.

Speed flying in the French Alps

SPEED FLYING

Speed flying takes place in the mountains. It is a mix of skiing and paragliding. This is a sport for experts only!

Speed fliers use small paragliders and wear skis. They skim down the mountainsides less than a metre above the ground.

HANG-GLIDING & PARAGLIDING

Hang-gliders sometimes fly in downhill races called speed gliding.

The pilot launches a glider from a ramp and races down the mountain. They must pass underneath and between gates.

Speed gliders travel up to 130 kilometres per hour!

Competition speed flying

Speed flying is thrilling but very dangerous.

RECORD BREAKERS

There are three main types of records: distance and out-and-return distance, speed round a course and gain of height.

Kari Castle and Davis Straub. Davis holds the record for rigid hang-gliders (class 5) at 655 kilometres

HANG-GLIDING & PARAGLIDING

The records for gliding are kept at the headquarters of the World Air Sports Federation in Switzerland

• The women's hang-gliding record is 402 kilometres, set by Kari Castle of the USA.

• The longest paraglider flight is by Will Gadd of Canada, at 423 kilometres.

• The gain-of-height record for paragliders was set by Englishman Rob Whittall in 1993. His gain was 4.5 kilometres!

Rob Whittall was the youngest person to be hang-gliding world champion at the age of 20 in 1989

CHAPTER 6: PEOPLE

AND PLACES

Some pilots know no limits to making gliding even more extreme.

AN ADVENTURE

French couple Zeb Roche and Claire Bernier set themselves an adventurous task. They decided to fly off the tops of the highest mountains in each of the seven continents of the world.

*Zeb Roche
and Claire
Bernier,
Mount
Everest*

Tandem paraglider

Flying as a passenger
in a two-seat
paraglider (a
tandem) can be
a good way to
experience gliding
for the first time.

Zeb and Claire are talented paragliders.
It took them almost six years to complete their task.
They set off in 1996 using a two-seat paraglider.

AMAZING STUNTS

Felix and Raul Rodriguez are stars of paragliding acro. They are world-famous for their solo and pair performances.

Mike Küng

Austrian Mike Küng is one of the bravest pilots in the world.

Mike broke the height record in 2004 when he launched from a balloon at 10,100 metres. He needed an oxygen mask, and was covered in two centimetres of ice!

Mike Küng launching himself out of a hot-air balloon

John Heiney performing a loop

John Heiney

American John Heiney holds the record for the most consecutive loops with a hang-glider.

QUESTIONS AND ANSWERS

Noel Whittall has been hang-gliding since 1973.

Noel Whittall

Do birds ever fly near when you hang-glide?

Yes. Quite frequently. Birds also play an important role, because they look for thermals. Spotting a soaring bird indicates good lift to a pilot.

What was the scariest situation for you in a hang-glider?

When I went to hang-glide in mountainous Austria. On my second flight, I found some good lift and stayed in it. For some time I just paid attention to my variometer. Then, when I took a look at my surroundings, I was hit by fear.

I had climbed above a whole mountain range! I was probably 3,658 metres in the air. The fear was overwhelming.

Glossary

Acro Short for aerobatics; loops, spins, wing-overs and other aerial stunts performed with a paraglider.

Altimeter An instrument that shows the height of a glider.

Battens The stiffening ribs used for wings.

Brakes The control lines of a paraglider.

Cells The individual divisions that make up a paraglider wing.

Control frame The triangular frame that the pilot use to control the glider.

Gliding The sport of unpowered flying that uses thermals and other forms of natural lift.

GPS Global Positioning System. An instrument similar to a car's satnav.

Joystick An aircraft control lever used on the Swift.

Keel The tube running down the middle of the hang-glider.

Leading edge The front edge of a glider wing.

Lift Rising air. Also used to describe the power generated by a wing moving through the air.

Microlight tug A small light aircraft with up to two seats that is used to launch gliders by towing them into the air.

Ram-air effect The way in which a paraglider wing keeps its shape.

Risers The straps between a paraglider's lines and the harness.

Rogallo An early hang-glider named after Dr Francis Rogallo.

Spoilers The flaps on top of a wing that stop the lift, making a glider turn.

Thermals The upward currents of warm air that are used by birds and gliders to gain height.

Trailing edge The rear edge of a glider wing.

Variometer An instrument that shows whether a glider is climbing or sinking. It is essential for all gliders, because it is impossible to tell whether you are going up or down once you are hundreds of metres above the ground.

Index